Copyright 2020 Somu Sivaramakrishnan

All the rights are reserved. No part of this book may be reproduced or transmitted in any form or by any means, electronic or mechanical, including photocopying, recording or by any information storage and retrieval system without written permission of the publisher, except for the inclusion of brief quotations in a review.

Thank you for all your understanding and support.

Author:

A simple fellow soul who believes in, completely rational, eternal, and heavenly happiness can be plausible for all. Starting from You!

Irrespective of who we are, it would greatly help us understand the most Reasonable and the most Useful divine concepts like Soul. Importantly reap benefits of it personally and for all.

We all seek for, more blissful, meaningful, reliable, and sustainable everyday life, starting from our own self. Understanding of the commonly misunderstood and unclear relationships among all the existences provides us greatly profound functional wisdom. Logically, it could also be the simplest path for Exponential Pleasure for all.

Reasonable and pure Goodness is Eternal! All the Souls, knowingly and unknowingly, seek for the Eternal Happiness!

Every day we make numerous decisions on various solutions towards seeking and solving problems. It could be personal, social, professional, small or big, or any number of sorts of problems. In the end, irrespective of any of our beliefs and deeds, it should settle in expected or unexpected. In fact, Any Outcomes that initially that cannot be Known.

Anything considerable we do could lead to search for one or more solutions. It could be one attempt, or many attempts to solve a problem successfully. Sometimes it could be endless attempts to solve a problem, still without a sensible, significant, substantial, and sustainable resolution.

In simple, for better solutions, we should ask ourselves some important questions.

Like, Are we looking at all the important Facts and Resources?

Are we communicating Explicitly, and confirming the Understanding with realistic expectations. Primarily and essentially as unclear communication could lead to Utter Failures that supposed to be Completely Thriving Success?

Are we ALL participating and contributing realistically?

Are we using the most Reasoning timely possible?

Are we receiving Reliable outcomes, even if minimally, progressively?

Are we creating solutions that can be factually Verified and Sustained?

Are we truly Learning and implementing consistently?

Are we trying to framework Compassionately equitable, Comprehensively streamlined, Sincerely strategic, and further more. All in the end, meaningfully and dependably help All.

When we attempt to solve a problem with Complete Inclusivity in as many aspects as reasonably possible, we could create thriving Solutions. When we focus on Completeness, better understanding of Souls could be vital. It would lead us to creating best of the Sustainable solutions. Essentially as it would benefit, praise, raise, and include All involved. Significantly because it would be Willingly, and especially Respectfully inclusive.

Briefly, when we believe in Soul Solutions and act on, it would greatly benefit. In simple, it would be by Respecting and Offering Reasonable Goodness for all, and Rationally Requiring the same from all involved. When it is followed consistently, it would lead to lasting success, peace and pleasure for all.

It is about every single individual's happiness starting from our own

self. We could achieve More Goodness Harmoniously, even at times, if it is not that obvious for us. When thoughtfully analyzed and recognized, it would be apparent that we would undoubtedly receive More Consequential Happiness. Profoundly, it would be instantly and over time.

We all desire, pray for, and produce goodness, at our own levels. It is also for lasting contentment, for now and for ever. It is great. At the same time, we might need to try it some more reasonably and realistically.

Some of us might ask, How can we even define Goodness as it could differ for different people and groups? Correct, it is not easy. Well, for true, it might meaningfully, mutually and beneficially take considerable efforts. We could focus on facts, outcomes, pros and cons so far. In its completeness, and work on it as a group, we would find out more and more gradually, about True Goodness.

Especially, we must start try to practice it, whenever and wherever plausible. In numerous aspects, it would directly and indirectly, make our own lives more in peace and pleasurable.

At any level feasible, we must try to attain Complete Goodness - given the circumstances. Importantly then on, carry it afterwards equitably. We must rationally help each other as we are helping our own selves. Naturally or at least for our own Unexplainable Soul's Goodness that Pushes for the Hidden Eternal Happiness.

It is a journey. We must attempt to properly realize and understand. If we do so, for even small Goodness we produce, we forward ourselves to further True Inner Joy. That we cannot even conceive or articulate.

Along the way, we might even make some mistakes. Unfortunately and unknowingly some sins too. For reliable happiness, that need not stop the Soul's - Goodness Journey. Consciously, recognize the mistakes, forgive yourself, request for forgiveness, correct rationally, and move on.

Wisely, steadily, and consistently, we would start creating more and more Goodness. If we could, we would relish completely cheerful, sustainable, and heavenly happiness. Such great pleasure would be, for this life and beyond - if you believe in it.

We have got All and Beyond to create such blissful state. But the *willingness* of those souls that feasibly can. Also, the contribution of ALL involved, sensibly with No Exceptions. This would accomplish the state of Conclusive Truth - Remarkably Phenomenal and Timeless Happiness.

When it transpires, it would be YOU the first to relish the true joyfulness. As you are the one in this conversation, and willing to do the best for yourself. Along with you everyone will join you harmoniously. It is completely feasible.

End of the Soul Solution Search for reasonable common problems and sufferings. The Dawn of the Complete Eternal Bliss for All - Starting from You!

Thank you! Have a Great Day-Every Day!

Sincerely - A Fellow Soul,
Somu Sivaramakrishnan

CONTENTS

Prologue **12**

Structure of the Book 15

Primary Sources of the Contents 17

Acknowledgements **19**

Soul **20**

What are some of the basics of Souls that I can use? 36

What if someone tells my beliefs are wrong? How to over come such situation? 43

How can I be sure, if my beliefs are True and Good, to progress and evolve my Soul? 48

Am I a Good Soul? Can I be one? 52

Prologue

Welcome and Thank you for joining me in this Conversation. In this short journey with a fellow-soul, let's mutually find out, how a completely reasonable, harmonious, goodness, and happiness filled life can be real and plausible. Not just for Us, but for All Souls, Irrespective of any of our current believes. **Especially, in a profound way, observe, discover, realize, and enjoy that you are the most valuable soul that exists.** Who also deserves the most blissful happiness - in a very profound and positive way.

"Really?!"

I think so. Let's briefly explore.

Well, The exceptionally uninvited wander - when in it. Wondering the very existence - when walk it. It could be a blessing - when done it. The overwhelming that you strive to overcome, over and over that led to this Soul Solution Search journey.

Especially, resolve to critical problems. An attempt, for making the soul's walk-the-walk, in this life and plausibly beyond - a pleasant good fortune! When received, such consistently evolving extreme opportunities, revealed Patterns that could alleviate and resolve.

They are the Reasonable Patterns that could produce best of the solutions, for all the problems.

Initially it may not be evident. Though, it would resolve for every single problem that we face every day. **More reasonably - at least for the most problems that we face, the most reasonable, rewarding, and harmonious solutions exist.** Notably, it benefits the entirety. This peaceful and pleasureful state can be achieved by Promoting, Reliable and Rational Goodness that Sustains.

In brief, the patterns recommend that all starts from individuals and their own seeking for happiness. Irrespective of the numerous believes that we may have, if we are not here, it would make no sense at all. Assume, if we are not here, we would not even know or realize, the existence of anything here, or anywhere.

Our existence is the most important and our own happiness is the paramount for each of us. How we achieve such, possibly sustainable happiness, could differ among us. Still YOU are the most important in this short journey. Right here and right now, you are the one who could deserve the very bests of the eternal bliss - tangibly and profoundly.

Structure of the Book

In this book of, 'Soul Solution Search Series - 101 to 777! Discussion and Solution on common complex questions!', this is Edition 1. A Short TOPIC Book, that converses on "Soul ".

These series of books on 'Soul Solution Search' would be released like this Short TOPIC Books. Also, there would be Combined-TOPICS Books that would speak on various topics. This would be for more and better understanding of the Soul's eternal journey.

Each Topic would start with adequate level of introduction. Where appropriate, also some of common questions, answers and reasonable solutions would be discussed. The contents may start at simple levels, so that it would be easy for the common readers. The conversation would evolve from there.

Further, it would grow based on the flow, needs, interests received, and beyond. Each Edition would be expanded with appropriate and considerably enriched contents.

For Readers who may be interested in Specific TOPIC, separate 'Short TOPIC Book' would be released. These Short TOPIC Books will have some of common conversations, and specific substance furnished for better understanding.

Primary Sources of the Contents

Contents of these Series of Books are primarily based on the vast extra ordinary personal experiences and opportunities that I received. They are both wonderfully also blissfully great, and terribly also awfully bad experiences.

I am very Thankful for all the wealth of experiences. Though, I greatly prefer those that make the situation better for all involved. More importantly, Self motivated Soul Solution

Search for specific problems, and self-interpretations of everyday wisdom from all fellow-souls like you. My heartily honor, appreciation, and Thanks for that. Thank you!

Further, if anyone finds any of the content as inappropriate in anyways, please forgive me. Please note that the intent of the content is to promote Reasonable, Sustainable, Completely Inclusive - Goodness based Happiness for All.

Acknowledgements

Thanks for my **Parents** for bringing me to this Great World,
Thanks for my Great **Friends** for teaching me to Think Good,
Thanks for my **Family** for their extended support during Toughest Times,
and **Special Thanks for You** for accompanying me in this Brief Journey!

Further, I would like to extend my Thanks for those who unknowingly hurt me. I pray for their souls also. I Thank them because, as those who did Right for me Taught me how to be Good like them, those who did wrong to me Taught me how I should not be. It's an important learning that made me to Search for Good Solutions and Answers. I believe, that made me a better Soul. They are very vital part of the truth and the Journey of the Souls. I wish that they realize and correct me and correct themselves. So, I Thank them!

Additionally, my Thanks for Everyone, Everything and Nothing - All the Souls!

Soul

Dear Good Soul. Foremost, Thank you for accompanying me in this brief journey.

"Really?! How do you even know that I am a Good Soul?", you may ask.

Well, as we start this brief journey, where I know nothing about you. I wanted to positively assume something Good about you. So, I assumed and addressed you as Good Soul. I call this Positive-Prejudge-Enabling for the ease and please of the conversations.

Life that is made up of such pleasant simple things as, Thinking someone Good and Thanking someone for even small things. It makes the journey more beautiful and delightful. Feeling Thankful, sharing and expressing make it greatly pleasing for everyone involved. For the most, it ensures, enables and empowers to be happier, than if just be based on the materialistic circumstances.

Soul! Assume that your body is sitting comfortably and reading this book. If not, please make yourself comfortable. The environment is safe, at least some peace in mind, and reasonable for you. Thank you.

Now, when you comfortably read, your body is apparent and tangible. But someone is reading along with you that only you can realize. May be you call your consciousness or your self or any other names you may want to call. The part of you that is not physical, but had been, and will be with you FOREVER! For simplicity, let us call him / her / other as Soul - for now.

If you are an enquiring, empathetic, and compassionate soul, you can understand it better. If you cannot for now, do not worry. You will ultimately. Mostly, it cannot be expressed through articulation, but can only be understood through profound inner realizations. It is too insightful that it cannot easily to be explained to one another. More importantly, it is hard for anyone to ever make you Feel and Realize, it for yourselves in its Entirety. Gradually, you will know it for yourself.

Irrespective of who we are, it would be greatly fruitful to know about Souls. It would need open minded willingness, efforts, practices, and karma, to know it at reasonable level in this lifetime. It would be hard to make someone really teach, enable to realize, evaluate and understand it without one's own longing for it. If some one could, it would be very rare, through one of Truly Enlightened or trending to Great Souls.

It would be based on such Great Souls who display True and Explicit Values, and Practices - Not just through read knowledge. It is not just about knowledge, but primarily about Reasonable Practice. We need to be aware though, in recognizing a Good or a Great or an Enlightened Soul, from a less-than-standard soul.

No need for any compelling complex-sacrilege tests. But some basic levels of willingness and openness in the Good Soul conversation. It would be without need for, any negatively - comparing, conflicting, or concluding on one's views are better than the other's. Rather, through complacent mutual complements. Just pure seeking, asking, listening, possible mutual learning, consuming, benefiting, enjoying, and finally Thanking for each other.

Good Souls like us, start with believing in the other souls as Genuinely Good Souls. This positive-prejudge or assumptions greatly help us toward positively motivated results. At the same time, our Goodness and positive expectations could place us in some trouble. As it sometimes also give a few overly materialistic souls to take advantage of, in wrongful ways.

We must not think too much about the negativity irrationally. At the same time, we just need to be little more aware of such souls and scenarios. Further, quickly navigate to our Reasonable, Positive and Beneficial ways of living for all. It would be including those with negativities.

Understanding of souls could be the easiest when like minded souls interact. Otherwise, it could be extremely hard, strive to understand - even with complete determination, openness, and freewill. As it is not just about reading and understanding. But more importantly, requiring feeling beyond normal perceptions, presumptions, and practices.

Basic levels of fairness and empathy towards other souls, without constraints, felt and understood would greatly help. Understanding of such souls could be easier, otherwise could be extremely complex. For now, let us believe that your beliefs on the souls are the best - at least for yourself, and so their own for everyone. Let us be Content and Happy with it for now - peace for all in mind.

In certain, heavenly presence you could naturally be enabled to Feel and Understand the Soul for yourselves. Also some heavily pressured circumstances may also permit us tap into. In this case, we could understand the soul to some level. Apparently, one way is always preferred than the other.

Numerous diversified teachings and perceptions make understanding of the Souls more complicated. For example, some believe that the sinful Souls will vanish after life. Some others believe that the Blissful Souls will become one into peace.

Indeed, very complicated to comprehend. Especially because of the preconceptions, understanding, and complexities involved.

Common beliefs and assumptions that involve are vast. Further, unprecedented levels of diverse, and unclear premises to be navigated. As example,

* Souls are progressed after life by means of credentials, that lead to Heaven or

* The value of cumulative learning and accomplishments through unknown and uncountable lives. It is the profound Tests and Travel. That believed to end based on, the at most state of value that can be attained. Then it would eternally end, by becoming as part of the God Himself or Herself or Itself.

* Also sometimes conceived to become one with Nature, Everything and Nothing.

Complex for sure, if without some levels of, related knowledge and understanding.

* Just collective values of deeds, for known and unknown reasons. They are spent in this life that we live in. As we feel and know - right here and right now, or more deeply

* An Atom to the Universe and everything in between as we know in this life and beyond, known and unknown. They all have individual and collective Souls that Ever Exists. Every Soul has its Profound and Inconceivable Value. Cumulative Experience and Knowledge from an Ever Living Soul is Permanently Obscure during this life. A Soul's Value can only be, retrieved limited and understood hazily, for purposefully unknown reasons.

Relevant and fractional Soul's values are repossessed and forgotten during related triggers during this life. Even for non-beings. At freewill and importantly accidentally, a Soul's value can be enriched through a life time of Goodness produced. It is especially kept unknown for Good reasons.

A Soul's value could change based on ever single even inconceivable little deeds and things that occur. As result, subatomic level consequences and domino effects are evaluated and calculated that are Complete. The Completeness of the calculations and protecting them are beyond life as we know it. The methods of calculations used are unimaginable and haze at best.

There is simplicity in this complex context of understanding of the Souls. It is that, just by being **Reasonably and Consistently Good could fetch all the bliss.** It could reward with unthinkably greater eternal happiness. In this conception, all is very well captured and recorded. In its entirety utilized for more Good to be produced for now and beyond this life. In brief, **What goes around Exponentially comes around with complete reasoning!** Or Simply

* Rejected as, "There is nothing as Soul exists at all", or many more such - BELIEFs!

They are just BELIEFs that could be diversified and difficult to realize. Especially, it is hard to understand, from the perspectives of the others. In extreme circumstances, for some closed individuals and groups, understanding could further be exceedingly hard. It is because they are not simplified for them. Also, sometimes they do not allow, entertain or believe in such opportunities. Because for simple self satisfaction, worry of punishment for considered sacrilege, or the benefit of very small groups who seldom even benefit from it. So, it is still hard and unnecessarily-complex for the unfortunate-innocents. When referred with respect, empathy and Goodness.

Ultimately, it supposed to be meaningful-differences of various kinds. Instead of supporting and benefiting towards broadened-blessed-blissfulness, as misunderstood, it unfortunately hurts the mutual-harmony.

For some, it may seem like the discussion on the Soul somehow tending to discuss on religion. It is common perception. They both are in general discussed mostly related and have similar kinds of scenarios applicable. So it could be perceived in such way.

When it gets to religion, in general, it gets more intensive. It is a common and reasonable understanding that Good Souls believe and support mutual respect and acceptance. Especially, keeping precious personal beliefs respectfully with in. At the same time, respecting others ideas, either understood, misunderstood or amalgamated. Beliefs are reasonably, respected, and accepted by Good Souls. Provided it can reasonably produce goodness without creating conflicts. Also, make someone feel hurt as sacrilege to their reasonable beliefs, intention to deceive, or such below standard acts.

Good human souls also believe in Soul, God, Religion, and such divineness. They also believe that their beliefs offer great common values and goodness. It is not considered a big barrier for them to comfort, love and help those with other beliefs.

For such Good Souls, it is respectful and acceptable, when an idea can deliver Goodness and Happiness for all. Though they may heartily praise and love, their own beloved God and Religion that bring eventual pleasant structure in to their lives.

Different believes preach different ideas, based on its own evolution, and countless historic circumstances. Good souls take the reasonable goodness from it. A simple starting solution towards mutual understanding, harmony and happiness could be, to simply respect each others beliefs.

Initially some might be worried to respect others beliefs as they praise and protect their own beliefs. This is completely reasonable and understandable. If we truly wish that our own beliefs to be understood, respected and praised by others then at least understandably we need to be assistive.

For mutual harmony and fruitfulness, it would be reasonable that we may also be willing to be flexible in a supportive way. It is not that one to follow the other. But for eventual and considerable mutual benefits, both to just respect each others views harmoniously.

Ultimately, the informed souls would recognize that all different beliefs are tending to, in the end towards, ideas for happier life experience. If you will such happiness even beyond life as we could feel and know it.

When discussed, it is believed by the Good Souls that some of simple, good, and diversified knowledge profoundly helps. Understanding and using them in every day life, contributes, comforts, and evolves their own good beliefs, at various levels. It enriches towards more profound and eternally genuine Goodness, and Happiness.

Eventually, for different individuals, the level at which it could be understood, and felt might vary. It would be based on the circumstances and the understanding of the individual that seeks, or the group that discusses.

Especially, the understanding and benefit would be higher, when such discussion can be genuinely open and sensible. Ultimately, it would more beneficially progress them, in their own beliefs with more reasoning and respect. Progressing to Profound Happiness!

What are some of the basics of Souls that I can use?

Great! If you asked this or similar questions or something around this thought cheers for yourselves. Irrespective of beliefs or ways-of-lives followed, day-by-day Great things on learning about Souls and using it appropriately are recognized. These realizations are both explicit and within, towards greater blissful life experience, and especially towards common Good.

At least for this non-critical conversation, simply to start with, make sure that you rationally help yourselves and others. Reasonable Goodness is Eternal Happiness. Feel Good, and be Happy about anything and everything that you have got. Respect everyone and everything you come across. Do not waste food and other vital needs. Instead as much as plausible, give it to someone in need.

Meaningful understanding of Soul is Not just about the most knowledge about it. But it is about Deeds, even small and Sensible Goodness that is produced in everyday life.

Try to empathize and assist any and all souls you encounter. Especially, when received opportunities to help needy of different basic necessities - act up on as much as plausible.

Recognize that every moment is unique and precious that never repeats. Praise it and use it to the best, for yourselves and for all.

Pay attention to the 'Present' and admire the current blessings and opportunities around you. Please do the most rational Good you can, as that is the most precious for your Soul.

Be attentive to other human, all beings, and even non-beings. Realize and respect that everything around you, anywhere and everywhere is there to teach something. Importantly learn from you.

Do realize your importance. Be kind to your own realistic Goodness and Happiness. Unless well thought through thoroughly and made sure, you do not have to hurt yourself doing any Good. Just try to do Good, as much as you can at reasonable levels. This is because, reasonable levels of goodness would make it more pleasant, and take it a long way further and lasting.

Avoid bad. When you cannot avoid defending bad, you could get hurt. Testing the Soul is part of the Soul's evolution. You will face all kinds of tough situations, manage and survive. By all Good means, strive to at least Survive. With Reasoning, possibly and amicably, try to end any bad for anyone as soon as possible. Bad in the name of nothing is good. Bad is bad and never good for none.

You may ask then how would we experience any bad. No worries! Along the way naturally as Good, bad shall try to come across. No one need to create any bad, it shall find its own way. When you face it, try to solve it for everyone's good.

Some may be obvious and some others can be completely obscure. Try not to fall for fakes. It is important to realize that you want to help everyone and every thing you encounter - Starting from yourself.

Aware of what you wish for. Keep it simple, Good and Cheerful. Thoughts and prayers have far too impacts to your Soul, and its outcomes. Make all the prioritized wishes, at your inner soul level, as deep as you could realize with in you. Like a conscious-heartfelt prayer. Soul travels far, be patient - reasonably. When appropriate it would reveal it self and bring the best for you.

When you could understand and realize, you would know, the depth and reasoning of the presently inconceivable. For those who are not familiar, it could be extremely profound and complex. If complicated, you need not worry too much about Soul and other such ideas. Rationally, it could seem complex.

Especially based on, the current place of the Soul in the eternal journey that is unthinkable and unrealizable for the most. Just continue learning at your own comfort. Practically for now, it would be easier and better, at whatever levels possible, Reasonably Think Good and Consistently Do Good. It would be one of the most satisfying, joyful, and natural path to learning about Soul.

Simple, Explicit, and Reasonable Goodness is the most lasting of all. It could sustainably help your Soul to evolve at a reasonable phase.

At a minimal level, make sure that you are reasonably Happy with at least minimum basic needs and if possible wants. Help others to pursue and have it. Nevertheless, try always to go beyond at reasonable levels, to further progress and succeed. As you could do more good with it. In turn, bring more pleasure for all Souls around you, including yourselves.

Propagate the Goodness and Happiness across - at whatever and all levels possible.

These are some of the simple, practical and Good ways to enrich your Soul.

If it is complex, please, do not worry much. When the right circumstances and time occur, you, they, everyone and everything, needless-to-ask, would know it all. The truth about the Soul will completely unfold to Permanent-Blissful-Happiness.

What if someone tells my beliefs are wrong? How to over come such situation?

If someone tells you, whatever your beliefs - they are wrong. First of all, you do not need to argue or get angry. Those who especially overly argue and fight to prove something are only those ignorant innocents. Who do not understand or did not get opportunity to understand the truth of, the richness and the relationships among the souls. They did not learn about the reasons for the vital existence of the various different kinds and believes.

In very simple thoughts, otherwise we all could be robots that know the same. No new Learning that could help. Unless we create such Good ones in the Heavens, and give life for it! No new ways of Feeling Happier to eternity, thus no purpose to exist. This simply is based on current common thoughts and rational understanding.

Second of all, please comfort your Good selves that those individuals could be little more open minded and move on.

Most importantly, please realize that the same could be felt at the other end, as well. So please empathize, and try to be little more open minded for your selves. Truly, try to start realizing and relishing at least some of the Goodness from the others perspectives.

Please realize that every single thing ever existed, exists, and will exist has purpose and something to learn from it. In fact, implicitly it's trying to relate itself with you and learn from you that you yet to realize. There is nothing wrong in learning some Good from somewhere and anywhere. Especially, if that can benefit you and everyone around you. With such a profound understanding, if you do not wish, you do not need to be explicit about it. Particularly, if in a conflicting scenario.

As however believed, it is your own Soul's journey. Keep it as peaceful and pleasant for yourselves as possible. Your Soul will teach and learn all along its journey. In simple, try to reasonably do Good for yourself, and for all.

The open minded new learning is important. As this would only assure more happiness when understood properly and approached as part of the progress of the soul.

Also this purification of your inner soul would only make it a pleasant dwelling place for whichever the God of yours or other beliefs. As it becomes, more and more meaningfully good. The almighty would rest time-to-time, and ultimately, eternally with Glory and Smile. Pure Souls never offend any for any reasonable reason. So, your Good Religious or any other Good beliefs. Praise it and be happy!

Third of all, you would know all you need to and feel little better. You might sensibly respect and agree with the other person or group, on at least some of their Good beliefs. This would be even though they may or may not agree with your Good beliefs. It would take realistic situational time. This approach would genuinely produce Goodness for all.

This is where you prove to be a Better Soul. Not than them as it should only increase conflicts and negativity. But than whom you were a short while ago. This is a natural, simple, and pleasantly profound response.

As an example, this further purifies your Good Soul. By doing so, you made your own God bless, love and believe in your Good Soul, more than ever before.

This could further progress your Soul - in the path to an Enlightened Soul! Obviously, not so simple, but at least, give some valuable credit for your Good, Courteous and Friendly soul. This is more profound than just knowing every single verse in any Good script - without practicing it towards Common Good.

There could be many such steps taken to help you at that and such complex situations. You may already be doing most of all these and beyond by yourselves. If so, I wish this conversation would further emphasize your Goodness. Further, progress your Great Soul for an amazingly expanded better Soul.

How can I be sure, if my beliefs are True and Good, to progress and evolve my Soul?

Since no one knows about what exactly is Soul that can tangibly be proved for all. Every question and conversation is a contribution that progresses to more meaningful understanding of it. Here your contribution must be appreciated. Thank you.

How everything works around it is also all different perspectives, ideas, beliefs, or so. As equally as others, yours could be right.

You consider, learn, accept, use, relish and practice, reasonably profound cumulative teachings. This could be from the Great Souls of the past and the present. Amalgamated and unrecognizably grouped. May be yours could be one such. I thank you for your contribution.

Just follow the goodness in what you have, right here and right now, and progress reasonably.

In fact, if you will, you could learn from all the good opportunities. Make a very pleasant, positive and progressive one out of them. For your own soul to start with, when you had the question to start from. This could help you and all around you. Provided it makes sense for you. Possibly produce consciously mindful goodness for all.

This would be very similar to, how you made your own happy life. At least, seeking and trying to make one. Profoundly, it is from all the opportunities that you came across, so far. Further your own consciously thoughtful contributions.

It is just that in this ever rapidly evolving world, it is like you personalized your beliefs with the core values untouched. This would feel more comfortable for your own beliefs. Further with more mindfulness, reasonability, goodness, and blissfulness.

Please note that you did this basic change for your own rational satisfaction and better understanding. Now, without any reasonable sacrilege, follow your regular beliefs with confidence, pleasure and fulfillment. In fact, it could make you more realistic and respectful for your own current beliefs. Follow it, producing more goodness and progress.

Most importantly, please consciously make sure that in simple, you are happier. Not bothering any of the basic constructs around you. You are enabling others around to be happier and rationally friendlier with you.

Feeling blessed with that content move on with cheers. The easier and obvious it could be, it would increase happiness steadily and assist the best for all.

Knowing that with your beliefs, learning and cognizant leaning, you are able to reasonably produce greater Good for yourself. Perhaps sensibly might help the most. It could even be gracefully serve all - Delightfully!

Am I a Good Soul? Can I be one?

Believe it or not, whoever you are, and whatever you did then and do now - You are a Good Soul! If you believe that you are not a Good Soul. It may be based on your own mistakes and sins that you may only know. It is unfortunate that you came to such belief of suffering, and wrongful conclusion.

You used your own interpretations and judgment. Now, you may briefly whisper to yourselves that you are a Good soul. At least, you are in the process of going to be a Very Good one, for sure. Just More Reasonably Work on it.

Towards the truth, if you will, further you may gratify yourselves. In the longest Soul's journey, you will ultimately become a Great Soul. You can and you will become such Great Soul as someone that you always admired from the bottom of your Soul.

If you further will, ultimately you will become a far better Soul. Even better than anyone, even The Greatest soul, you never even heard of. Only positively!

Complicated for sure. Just leave it, until you could become one such and realize for yourselves. You would be proud that you could respect all around you the most, and be helpful and happiest the most.

Firstly, Believe in your Belief on Soul! Imagination is your limitation. But never forget or stop producing reasonable goodness and happiness for your self and all around you.

If you believe in Nothing. It is just a lack of realization that you still are believing in a Thing that you call NoThing! So profoundly you have to work for everything starting from a construct to all that you want to be, and work for it.

If you believe only in yourself, none other, and nothing else, then think of the most sustainable happiness for ever. Just, you have to work on everything for it, to reasonably achieve it, with your own framework.

If you believe in a God or an almighty, you are blessed with a reasonable framework. You would reason for yourself, to be the most helpful and the happiest, with in that constructs. Still you have to work with such beliefs to earn, deserve, and receive the very best, through your own God's blessings.

Whichever be your case, be happy that you believe in something that makes you happy. Also, make sure that your beliefs and deeds do not bother others.

For Good and bad, in a rational, as well as a worst case scenario, there must be Justifiable Consequences for every single deed. Realistically, no one can know that for sure.

Nevertheless, logically contemplating, as part of its basic construct and framework, there should be Profound Need for flaws. It would be understood, when it is appropriate, during the truly eternal journey of all the Souls.

Irrespective of it and whatever may have happened so far in anyone's life. The future is the most important and paramount. As it CAN be far better but the past cannot be. This can be even true for the most accomplished. As the past could have been Great at the same time the Future could be Far Better.

Finally, now, we believe in you that you are a Wonderful Good Soul. For the life to come, we wish and thank you for sustainably and reasonably producing Goodness and Happiness. Especially, when you create delight, not just for yourselves, and plausibly also for, all around you.

With the Glory of the Almighty let us flourish. With your kindness let us extend. With such contribution from All - True Heaven!

Let us create, The Completely Loving Eternal Blissfulness, for this life and beyond!

Thank you for exploring eternity, for your generous, gracious and compassionate - brief journey with me!

Have a Great Day - Every Day!

www.ingramcontent.com/pod-product-compliance
Lightning Source LLC
Chambersburg PA
CBHW051704040426
42446CB00009B/1294